# THE MONO BOX
## presents
# PLAYSTART 2
### Short plays from new voices

**Cold Feet and Bacon Sandwiches** by Kiran Benawra

**Meatballs** by Maatin Patel

**When the Leaves Fall** by Grace Tarr

**One Of The Good Ones** by Vivian Xie

OBERON BOOKS
LONDON

WWW.OBERONBOOKS.COM

First published in 2019 by Oberon Books Ltd
521 Caledonian Road, London N7 9RH
Tel: +44 (0) 20 7607 3637 / Fax: +44 (0) 20 7607 3629
e-mail: info@oberonbooks.com
www.oberonbooks.com

PB ISBN: 9781786829207
E ISBN: 9781786829214

Cover photography by Mark Weinman

eBook conversion by Lapiz Digital Services, India.

10 9 8 7 6 5 4 3 2 1

# Contents

# Foreword

The best way to learn to make theatre is to see your work in front of an audience. That's the ethos at the heart of Playstart. Creating a 15 minutes play is just as hard as writing a mainstage epic: it requires the playwright to be rigorously concise in the telling of the story and the language. There are no production fireworks to hide behind - it's about the relationship between performance, language and audience. It's in this purity where you can really see whose writing and performances are shining through.

It's a privilege to be working with The Mono Box. Their generosity of spirit, the sense of opportunity that accompanies it, and their absolute commitment to ensuring we are telling stories by people from a broad range of backgrounds and life experiences are infectious and values Hampstead holds dear.

As arts courses soar in expense and it's harder and harder for new talent to support themselves when at the beginning of their careers, it's vital that those of us who can, create bridges into the theatre for those starting out. We need new stories, we need new blood in the theatre, we need to invest in the talent for the future, which is why we're honoured to be collaborating with The Mono Box in supporting the next generation of writers, performers and directors.

Roxana Silbert
Artistic Director, Hampstead Theatre

# Introduction

This year has been one of growth for The Mono Box. We were lucky enough to be offered a helping hand by Roxana Silbert who we both worked with in our early days at RSC. What started as a casual conversation with her in a Walthamstow nail salon, ended up with The Mono Box being appointed an Associate Company at Hampstead Theatre where Roxana had recently been appointed Artistic Director. Her desire to bring new audiences to Hampstead matched with our need for support. After years of making things happen with nothing apart from sheer tenacity, the kindness of our volunteers and a lot of love, Playstart immediately was able to mature.

The scheme in which we mentor 4 emerging writers, pair them with a director each and provide them with actors to cast, rehearsal space and professional mentorship is now in its third year. And whilst last year it was held in a heating-less warehouse in Bermondsey, this year it is being hosted in a real live venue with seats, snacks and toilets.

If you were to look up The Mono Box in the dictionary Playstart would be its definition. A programme designed to demystify the process of putting on your own theatre work with professional mentorship and resources to experiement, Playstart encourages emerging theatre people to take control of their own artistry. Playstart is The Mono Box through and through.

We are thrilled to be able to offer young writers, directors and actors the chance to collaborate and work together to create something from scratch in this new venue, but ultimately we are happy that our company is being recognised by the industry for bridging the lack of opportunities for those starting out. We need these voices. If they aren't listened to they might cease to exist and we can't have that, can we?

Polly Bennett and Joan Iyiola
*Co-Founders of The Mono Box*

# Creative Thoughts

It took me a while for the penny to drop. That co-directors Polly and Joan had judiciously named their emergent organization "The Mono Box" with reference to the *mono*logues they were fast growing in their collection. I had just got back from living in Spain, where "mono" means "monkey". And, as a fresh young theatre maker eager to offer workshops in high-octane (and apparently "European") playfulness, "The Monkey Box" suited me excellently. It still does.

In the last 6 years, I have developed a language of veritable "monkey" play through workshops and platforms I have piloted and developed with The Mono Box – in improvisation, devising, comedy, character, clown and applied theatre. My pleasure, confidence and growing capacity as a facilitator & theatre-maker are thanks to Polly and Joan's vision, humility, and delicious desire to take risks and empower voices in an industry that can be very unpredictable indeed.

As someone who works closely with, but not always inside the organization, I see how compassionately and dynamically it steps into the gaps in the industry. For young actors auditioning for drama school, or those who might not go; for those who want to continue their training and try something different; for those between projects and auditions and (yes, inevitable) rejections; for those wanting to write or direct for the first time. Or for those, like me, who have an idea for a workshop and would like to try it out somewhere.

We theatre makers occupy a liminal space, one in which we live a life in between, or at the edges of things – stories, jobs, places, cultures, the real and the make-believe, the performer and the person, the stage and the audience. For all this, it is exciting, precarious, adrenalin-fuelled, unpredictable, vulnerable, important, sometimes overvalued, more often undervalued, and really hard-work. We need to know where we can go to find support and stimulation, where we can free-fall and make mistakes, where we can lose ourselves to find ourselves again. I believe The Mono Box has your back.

Over the years, I have had many impassioned conversations with Joan and Polly about how The Mono Box can foster a more creatively empowering and equitable theatre industry, and I feel sure that we are not only living through a powerful shift of consciousness – even awakening – but that The Mono Box is contributing to it. With a strong team of patrons, board members, producers and volunteers, with a Can Do, Will Do, Must Do attitude, it seems that anything might be possible.

The organisation started as an itinerant library, supported by the Old Vic and The Jerwood Space; it now has its own workshop and library space at The Biscuit Factory in Bermondsey, transformed by its handcrafted M O N O bookshelves housing over 3,500 plays which have been donated over the years. It has recently become Associate Company at The Hampstead Theatre, through which it hopes to reach a wider network of members through the Creative Conversation panels, Speech Share Live and PLAYSTART 2019.

As for the workshops, I ran my first ever workshop with The Mono Box in a glorified shed in Brixton back in 2014 as part of a one-off pilot weekend. I had a lot of fun. Now there is an extensive rolling workshop programme, with a magnificent range of practitioners, as well as curated workshop weeks, including European Theatre Week in 2017, TOTAL Theatre Week in 2018 and Creative Acts in 2019.

The European Theatre Workshop Week is an excellent example of my relationship with The Mono Box. I had a wish for more international theatre workshops in London, and Polly and Joan said "Then we shall make it happen!" Supported by the Arts Council, I invited a whole host of European based practitioners to deliver workshops in Bouffon, Devising, Corporeal Mime, Viewpoints, Improvisation, Clown and Melodrama. The week had a profound impact on the organisation, expanding its sense of what it was capable of, and reaching out to a wider network of international theatre makers and performers based in London.

I may, by now, be biased, but The Mono Box is a place where I have seen anything and everything happen. I don't mean that lightly. In my own workshops, actors with little confidence in their creative voices have taken me to the inner recesses of their brilliant minds through exquisitely imaginative storytelling. I have seen performers who have lost their passion find it again, and I've seen powerful collaborations begin. I have seen buildings taken over and new plays performed and actors say - I'm no longer going to wait to be asked; I'm going to make it myself.

"PlayStart" is another judicious title for a scheme which provides a stand-out opportunity for new writers to start writing a play, but it serves as a strong metaphor for The Mono Box's ethos. It's where we can come to play. Not only start to, but to remember how to. And, crucially, to remember why we do this for a living.

As I see it, this apparent box has expanded and there are monkeys everywhere, eager to play and itch and scratch and explore what it is to be sort of human and sort of animal, and look at the world from upside down, inside out. Sometimes show their bottoms and eat bananas, if they so please. Which is all to say, The Mono Box is cutting the edges of theatre practice in a truly radical way, and it is a howling dream to be a part of. On we go.

Amy Gwilliam, 2019
*Theatre Maker*

# Creative Thoughts

Having worked with The Mono Box since its very beginning, I have seen it grow and become an indispensable resource for a huge range of theatre makers over the years. Through its commitment to continual training The Mono Box is a thriving community facilitating theatre people to develop their practice and find like-minded collaborators.

Artists, not least emerging artists, will often produce work themselves and create their own opportunities- usually underpinned by invaluable collaborations. This certainly comes with as many challenges as it does rewards. My own work as a director is reliant on play and fuelled by collaboration. With the people I collaborate with we're never finished working things out – mucking about and attempting to see where something can go. Similarly the The Mono Box's ethos, that is in the fabric of its new writing scheme, Playstart, provides a rare opportunity for writers, directors and actors to throw paint at the wall and actually do their chosen profession without the threat and pressure of completion or perfection. The Mono Box provides the much needed infrastructure within which teams can focus on their collaboration, develop their approach and interrogate their process. The Mono Box has recognised that the industry has a responsibility to allow writers, directors and actors to write, direct and act.

Playstart provides crucial opportunities for emerging directors to train on the job. Directing short plays is such fertile and rewarding ground to focus experimentation with their rehearsal process and evolve approaches to dramaturgy. For writers, directors and actors Playstart has become a way to share ideas, methods and practice across all disciplines, to explore the cross-over and generate a piece of work which would never be made without everyone involved and a properly holistic approach.

Having mentored the directors this year with Andrew Whyment, I have been thrilled to meet such dynamic and engaged artists. The knowledge that many of the plays and director/writer relationships of previous years have continued their lives beyond Playstart is testament to their solid foundations provided by Polly and Joan at The Mono Box. With the level of professional mentorship and guidance provided all through the process, Playstart provides directors, writers and actors with the vital space to make new work which I have no doubt we'll see more of in the future.

Ned Bennett
*Director*

# The Plays

*Cold Feet and Bacon Sandwiches*
Written by Kiran Benawra
Directed by Sibylla Kalid

Patient A – Zara Tomkinson
Patient B – Martha Pothen

*Meatballs*
Written by Maatin Patel
Directed by Ebe Bamboye

A – Ikky Elyas
B – Cassian Bilton
C – Lauren O'Leary
D – Isabel Adomakoh Young

*When the Leaves Fall*
Written by Grace Tarr
Directed by Evangeline Cullingworth

Max – Felix Pilgrim
Billie – Olivia Dowd
Shay – Risha Silvera

*One of the Good Ones*
Written by Vivian Xie
Directed by Adrian Tang

Elaine Chao – Angela Yeoh
Mitch McConnell – Christian Bradley

*Please note that these scripts may change before performance.*

Produced by Alison Holder for The Mono Box

Thank you to the following people for their wisdom and
support of these artists:

*Writer mentors*
Phoebe Éclair Powell, Ella Hickson,
James Graham and Vinay Patel

*Director mentors*
Ned Bennett and Andrew Whyment

*Assistant Producers*
Jessica Bastick-Vines and Harriet Taylor

*Assistant to Co-Directors*
Miles Sloman

and

Ann McNulty, Ruth O'Dowd, Mark Weinman,
Ingrid Mackinnon and Laura Dredger at MoveSpace,
Mark Maughan, and the entire team at Hampstead Theatre

# Writer Biographies

**Kiran Benawra**

Kiran is a writer and freelance assistant producer. She has worked on productions for BBC One, BBC Two and MTV, and she is also the creator of Channel 4's online comedy entertainment series, Rage Room. Kiran has an MA in Screenwriting and Playwriting. Her TV pilot script was included in the BFI Postroom's Top Picks of 2016. Kiran has completed the Soho Theatre Stand Up Comedy Lab, and she was a finalist in the comedy writing category at the Funny Women Awards 2017. She performs improv at the Free Association as part of the house team Dream Phone.

**Maatin Patel**

Maatin is a writer from London. He comes from a career in political campaigning and activism, which he's discovering is not as alien to the world of theatre as he once imagined! His involvement in anti-racism work informs a desire to affect change in the dramatic arts, in part by continuing to expand storytelling by and about people of colour. He hopes to contribute positively to that need through his own writing. Maatin is currently completing an MFA in Writing at Royal Central School of Speech and Drama. *Meatballs* is his first play.

**Grace Tarr**

Grace is a writer and actor. She trained at the London Academy of Music and Dramatic Art. Whilst there she began writing poetry and co-wrote and performed in What The Feminist?! a comedy sketch musical about feminism. WTF?! went on to be performed at Katzpace, London, and the Edinburgh Fringe Festival 2018. Her first full length play Something Blue is currently being developed after scratch performances at The Nuffield Southampton Theatres. *When the Leaves Fall* is her first published play.

**Vivian Xie**

Vivian is a writer, comedian and museum frequenter from Toronto. She studied English literature and chemistry at the University of Toronto and is a graduate of The Royal Central School of Speech and Drama's MA Writing for Stage and Broadcast Media course. As a comedian, she is associated with the Soho Theatre Young Company and queer stand-up comedy group Mumsn*t Comedy Collective. Her work has been staged in Canada and the U.K. She misses home but calls her parents every night. She'd like to thank them, her friends here and elsewhere and Oscar Wilde.

COLD FEET AND BACON SANDWICHES
BY KIRAN BENAWRA

# Character List

Note: A & B can be played by actors of any
gender or race.

A loves bacon sandwiches and is in a coma.
A laid-back lovesick foodie, A is a calming
influence but their brave face cracks when they
get some surprising news.

B has cold feet and is in a coma. Anxious and
depressed, loving and ambitious, B tries to
deflect emotions with humour but struggles to
keep it together when faced with A's change in
circumstances.

*(Hooked up to IV drips, fashioning hospital gowns, A & B exist in a clinical setting. Their feet are bare.)*

A: If you were a vegetable, what type of vegetable would you be?

B: Hmm. An aubergine. Definitely an aubergine.

A: Why?

B: It's just a bit more unusual isn't it. You don't get many purple vegetables.

A: Beetroot.

B: Yes. But. That's salad.

A: Suppose. *(Pause.)* Well aren't you going to ask me?

B: Fine. If you were a vegetable, what type of vegetable would you be?

A: I don't really know to be honest.

B: I think you'd be a potato.

A: Why'd you say that?

B: People always forget potatoes are vegetables.

A: Poor potatoes.

   *(Silence.)*

A: So did that work?

B: What?

A: Make your toes feel a bit less itchy.

B: Oh no, now why would you say that?

A: I think your toenails are getting a bit long too.

B: So much for sleeping beauties.

A: My feet are actually quite cold.

B: Not as cold as mine.

A: I've heard the doctors talking to Bill again you know. They're going to pull my plug soon.

B: Did you try talking back this time?

A: No point.

B: If anyone came to visit me, I'd talk back.

A: We're just bodies in beds now. Our machines speak for us. All we can say is 'beep, beep, beep.' And our brains are, well, they're–

B: They are here. *(Pause.)* So did Bill say when he was going to, erm, do it?

A: Don't really know. It was hard to hear through the crying. I know I'm going to be cremated though.

B: Oh. I was quite looking forward to us being buried next to each other.

A: You what? Even if I was being put in a hole in the ground, why would they put you in the hole next door?

B: Well they might if you at least tried to speak up.

(Pause.)

A: The worms will eat you, you know.

B: What worms?

A: In the ground. If you're buried, they'll get you.

B: Do worms have teeth?

A: Yeah! I think. They're like those fish that eat at your feet, taking off the dead skin. Yeah it feels nice for a bit, tickles even, but leave your feet in for too long and they'll be gone.

B: Gone? No, no, I need my feet.

A: All gone. Foot-less. Footloose. Oh now that's a good film. I love Kevin Bacon. And I love bacon. I hope my cancer tastes like bacon.

B: Actually they're very cold now.

A: Rub them together.

B: Let me put them on yours.

A: Okay.

*(A & B put their feet together.)*

B: What do you mean you hope your cancer tastes like bacon?

A: That's what I mean.

B: Oh. Okay.

A: Well people eat placentas don't they? They eat livers and kidneys. Had an uncle who tried monkey brain once. I just wonder what it tastes like and whether everyone's cancer tastes the same.

B: Probably all tastes like chicken.

A: Maybe more like chicken pate. A poisonous spread for your organs. But then you realise you've used high fat poison instead of low fat poison, which doesn't taste as nice but lets you live longer, so you ask your surgeons to get their knife and carefully scrape the poison off. Bless them they do try.

B: Do they smell?

A: The surgeons?

B: My feet.

A: Oh. Yes.

B: No they don't!

A: It's okay. I like the smell. Reminds me of cheese. Blue cheese.

*(B takes their feet away.)*

B: I need a foot spa.

A: You can boil eggs in a foot spa you know.

B: You can boil your feet too.

A: At least then they wouldn't be cold.

B: Do you have cancer in the feet too?

A: No, hasn't spread there yet.

B: I wish it had.

A: Hey!

B: Then you couldn't hop off and leave me.

A: I'm not.

B: When did they say they were going to do it?

A: I don't know.

B: You do know. You're twiddling your drip. Which means you're lying. Which means you know. You can tell me. I'm a very strong person you know. It might actually be nice to get some peace and quiet. You do talk quite a bit, take up the air with your voice–

A: Now hang on—

B: It's a lovely voice but it can be loud. I expect you'll make a lot of noise when you go.

A: I don't think it'll hurt.

B: But it might. What if it really hurts and you're screaming and screaming. And then there's just silence and I'm left with the memory of your screams. And the fear. The fear from the knowledge that one day it'll be me screaming. Unless they never put me out of my misery. That's another kind of torture—

A: It's this afternoon. It's happening this afternoon.

*(Silence.)*

B: Well. That is very soon.

A: Exactly. So I don't really want to spend my last few hours arguing with you.

B: What should we do instead then?

A: You could teach me to ice skate.

B: I don't really feel like it. Maybe later.

A: Hello! I don't have a later. You did promise—

B: A pinkie swear, not a promise.

A: Even more binding than a promise.

B: Fine. Follow my lead.

*(B holds onto their IV drip, gliding across the space nervously at first and then gets into their stride. A tries – and fails - to copy B's movements and eventually stops to watch B who performs an elegant dance with their drip. In a world of their own, B suddenly trips and falls.)*

9

A: Are you okay?

B: I can't feel my feet.

A: Cold again?

B: No. They're not there. Gone. I've lost them. I told you I didn't want to. I can't ice skate anymore.

A: But you were amazing.

B: I was amazing when I had my feet.

A: You do have your feet here.

B: No. I've lost them. They've cut them off again. Cut me out of the car, cut my feet off. I was going to walk home. 'I'll give you a lift, not safe to walk' they said. Then I never walked again—

A: It was an accident.

B: All the doctors, they all wanted my feet, my career. My feet or my life? They're the same thing. The same! And my feet were used to cuts and bruises. They were. So there was no need to—they took them both. Left. Gone. Right. Gone.

Now that is, that is greedy. It's not fair.

*(B starts to hyperventilate. A takes B's feet in their hand.)*

A: Look. Look. They're here. I've got them. Your feet. I've got them.

B: If I was driving then at least it would've been my fault.

A: It wasn't anybody's fault. It's just life. Wrong place. Wrong time. A wrong turn.

We're all passengers in Life's car. We're tied down and blindfolded in the back seat and there's no GPS, and before you know it, Life has lost control of the wheel and boom out we go through the windshield. Life walks away unharmed and leaves us in a ditch by the side of the road. And then goes to get a drive through McDonalds. Now. Take some deep breaths. In and out. In and out.

*(B begins to calm down. A massages B's feet.)*

B: I think God's more into clean eating than burgers.

A: I didn't say God. I said Life. Do you believe in God?

B: I used to. I think so. I want to. Then I could blame him.

A: Her.

B: God is probably gender fluid.

A: A gender fluid entity with psychopathic tendencies. And ADHD. And acne.

B: Thank you. I'm okay now.

*(B takes their feet away.)*

A: Don't be embarrassed.

B: Look, it's your big day. We should focus on you.

A: Okay. But–

B: The last supper.

A: What?

B: You should have a last meal. You know, like on death row.

A: Oh, great.

B: What would you like?

A: Hmm. A sandwich please.

B: You could have anything you want.

A: I know.

B: Okay. Any specific sandwich?

A: A BLT.

B: One BLT coming up. Now we do take all the ingredients, blend them up until they form a big brown mush and then pipe it all through a tube, bypassing your tongue so you won't be able to taste the dish. Would that be okay?

A: Perfect.

B: You should feel it slopping its way into your drip now.

*(A closes their eyes and holds onto their IV drip as if trying to taste the sandwich.)*

A: During chemo Bill always made me a BLT. Said it was a good nutritious meal - carbs, protein, bit of fruit and veg. I made him a BLT before I left him.

B: Ran away-

A: It wasn't fair on him. To look after me. Didn't feel like a marriage. He was my babysitter. I had to set him free.

B: That kind of backfired, didn't it?

A: Yeah it did. But now he's setting himself free of me so it's fine. I should've told him in person, not just left him a note. And then left him.

B: Well you left him a sandwich too.

A: I told him I was going and there wasn't any point in following me because I didn't love him anymore. And I put it in writing for him to read over and over again.

B: You didn't mean it. He knows you were trying to make him hate you. You went about it completely wrong, by the way. You should've run over his mum. Or his dog. Or his penis.

A: I was walking down the street, tears running down my face, and then I heard the sirens. *(Imitates a siren.)* It was an ice cream van.

B: Ice cream vans don't sound like that.

A: I know! I've just heard so many ambulances drive by that I can't remember the sound an ice cream van makes anymore.

B: It's more of a- *(also imitates a siren. A gives B a look.)*

A: So, I heard the ice cream van and I just thought 'I've got cancer, I've left my husband, I deserve an ice cream. I deserve an ice cream!' The siren gave me a burst of energy. I saw the van start to drive away so I ran. And I ran. And then I was here. And I never got my 99 Flake.

B: *(sarcastic.) That's* the most upsetting part really. Not that you fell over and banged your head, not that it was a hankering for ice cream that got you here and not the cancer at all. It's kind of funny in a way I suppose.

A: Can I add a dessert onto my last supper?

B: I can see where this is going.

A: I'll have a 99 Flake please.

B: Fine.

   *(A closes their eyes and shivers a bit.)*

A: It's nice and cold.

B: Do you know what else is nice and cold?

A: *(Simultaneously.)* You.          B: *(Simultaneously.)* Me.

B: Do you believe in reincarnation?

A: No.

B: Can you come back as my feet?

A: And let you walk all over me?

B: No, to keep me grounded.

A: You'll be fine.

B: When you go I'll be alone with my thoughts. I won't
be fine. I'll be trapped. And I can't escape. There's just
endless space here and you fill up a lot of it right now–

A: Hey!

B: With your voice, I mean. You have a great voice – it's
happy and calming and a lot of nonsense, but sharp too.
And it cuts my thoughts, pushes them down. But now,
now, oh, I feel, I feel–

A: *(Singing.)* 'I feel it in my fingers. I feel my coma toes.'

B: Stop it. That's not funny.

A: I'll come back as your feet, okay?

B: Thank you.

A: When I go, it's not going to get that bad again. You won't
feel that bad again. You have your feet here.

B: Don't worry. If I feel bad, I'll just have to feel bad. There's
nothing I can really do about it here, nothing I can hurt
myself with here, is there? I can't make it stop.

A: Like you did before?

B: Well I tried. I don't regret it though. Because I met you.

*(Silence.)*

A: I can hear them in the room now.

B: Already?

A: Yeah. Listen. Underneath the beeping.

B: It's too soon. It must only be early afternoon.

A: This is a good thing. It's a good thing.

B: Do you think they're going to do prayers first?

A: I hope not.

B: Surely, they won't just turn you off. Would they? What are they saying?

A: I don't know.

B: They have to give you some warning. You can't just disappear. You won't just disappear, will you?

A: Maybe. I really don't know how it works.

B: No. I want you to stay. You can't leave. I won't even get a note to remember you by.

A: You don't need a note.

B: It's those doctors again. Taking everything away. Have they done it? I can hear beeping but I'm not sure if it's mine or yours. What do you think?

A: Can you just stop asking questions for a second?

*(A tries to hold it together. Silence. B stands by A, unsure what to do.)*

B: You know, I'm actually quite jealous.

A: You're lying.

B: I'm not. You're going to discover what else is out there. You're about to find out life's greatest mystery. Death.

15

*(Pause.)* And you still have your feet. Oh, how I wish I was you.

A: Yeah. I'm going on an adventure.

B: Exactly. An exciting journey.

A: An exciting sleep. *(Pause.)* I feel sick.

B: I had a cat.

A: Okay.

B: There's more.

A: I didn't think that was the end of the story.

B: Right. So, I had a cat and the cat got sick. And I had to take her to the vet. And she was really sick so I had to put her down. And it was like she knew and she kind of clawed at me and hissed. But then, when it was happening, she was very peaceful. I swear I even saw her smile.

A: Yeah?

B: Yes. So. It'll be fine.

A: It'll be fine.

B: Exactly.

A: Actually, I don't think I want to go.

B: No?

A: No. I've been trying to put on a brave face for you but now you're being annoying and making up pets.

B: I'm not.

A: What was the cat's name?

B: Cat-erine. Catherine. Cathy. She didn't have a name.

A: Oh god.

B: Okay fine, I didn't have a cat.

A: I wanted to go out gracefully, I did. But I can feel myself ready to crumble.

B: Think of apple crumble. You like apple crumble.

A: I'm never going to taste anything ever again. I'm never going to feel hungry or feel anything else. I'm never going to talk to you again.

B: I'll still talk to you. So, you can just listen instead for a change.

A: I can't do it.

B: You have to. It's just life remember.

A: No this is death.

B: It just happens. We can't control it.

A: Well I want to try. *(Shouting.)* Bill? Bill!

B: What are you doing?

A: I'm very politely asking my husband not to murder me. Bill!

B: *(Shouting.)* Bill!

A & B: *(Shouting.)* BILL!

B: Just speak to him.

A: Right. Now listen here Bill, I may be a vegetable but I'm your vegetable and I don't want to be chucked in the bin just because nobody thinks I look very good anymore. I still have nutrition Bill! Can you hear me? I don't want to go. Because where would I go? I don't mind it here. I may even like it. And if I do go there's no way of knowing that you'll be able to grow a new vegetable patch to love, you know. I could be it for you. And I'm sorry if that's a disappointment. But better to have tried the vegetable diet and failed than to have never tried it at all. I love you Bill, and I don't really want to leave you. At least now you can see me and I can hear you and we can be together in a way. Just hear me this once though, hear me. *(Listens.)* No, stop saying goodbye. Stop it!

B: I want you to know that you have been the greatest friend to me and I-

A: Don't you start as well.

B: I know you're scared. I'm scared too. But it's okay. I'll be with you. And you know what, I've decided that I'm going to be cremated too. Yes. I am. So that when my atoms are floating about in the air, I can look out for a dust shaped you and fly over. And then we can just pick up where we left off. Sod Bill. Because you are my soulmate.

A: Will you hold my hand?

*(B takes A's hand. Silence.)*

A: You have very clammy hands.

B: No I do not.

*(B goes to pull their hand away but A clutches on.)*

A: No. Don't let go.

*(A closes their eyes and takes a deep breath. B looks at A and then closes their eyes and takes a deep breath. They continue holding each other's hands tightly. Lights fade.)*

## END

MEATBALLS
BY MAATIN PATEL

# Character List

A – male, south Asian, Muslim

B – male, white

C – female, white

D – female, black

All characters are all of similar age, 25-30.

*Alfresco at an upscale Italian eatery, midway through dinner. A table with four chairs, all occupied by unidentifiable characters sitting hunched over in darkness. The only thing illuminated is a large plate of meatballs in tomato sauce in the middle, half eaten. We are inside A's memory of this occasion. This will become clear later on.*

*A sits upright, staring at the plate. He picks up his fork and moves it towards the meatballs, hovering over the plate and hesitating, before placing his fork back down again.*

A: No need to panic. Just grin and bear it. Get your head in the game. Three, two, one...

   *The others spring to life, laughing in unison. They cheers, sip, and lower their glasses.*

D: I don't mean to go on about it. But it's just not sitting right with me.

B: I'll tell you what's not sitting right. This food. Think it might be time to unbutton.

D: I should email my boss. I'm going to email my boss. I can email my boss, right?

C: It'll all get cleared up in the morning, I'm sure. And need I remind you, we're here to <u>celebrate</u>! The return of our long lost friend...

A: Don't be silly, it's not been that long!

B: Why've you been avoiding us?

A: I'm here, aren't I?

   *B slaps A on the back.*

B: And aren't we grateful.

C: … And as it so happens our other friend here got some great news at work today/

D: Some great. Some not-so-great/

*D picks up her phone, tapping and scrolling irritably.*

B: … And so she's paying for dinner!

*D looks up.*

D: *(To A)* Have they always been this cheap?

A: You don't know the half of it. *(beat)* Are you sure I'm not encroaching on your/

C: Don't be silly! We haven't done dinner in ages. And I've been wanting the two of you to meet.

A: Why's that?

C: You know, I just think you're both great people and would get on really well/

*D slams down her phone.*

D: Seriously! Just how much is it to ask to have my name spelled right?

B: K-I-N-G? There, I did it!

*D shoots B a look. They both know it's not her last name that gets misspelled.*

D: *(To B)* Really?

A: I actually had a similar experience once/

D: I heard. With your boss and the thing with the/

A: *(To B and C)* Why did you tell her that?

B: Because it's a hilarious story, obviously.

A: Not to me it's not.

C: Come on, you love that story!

*B and C laugh knowingly.*

D: They mix me up with the other black girl, too. You know there's literally one other one? And they still manage to 'confuse' us.

*D picks up her phone and starts typing.*

C: *(To D)* You really get mixed up with someone else? I can't imagine that.

A: Well believe it. It happens all the time. By mistake, on purpose… and then somehow they think they're being charming or something.

*D pauses, looks up.*

D: Maybe I should wait. I don't want to leave it but/

B: Why are you so bothered? People make typos all the time.

D: You wouldn't get it.

B: I'll have you know I get people's names wrong fairly often. It happens. Big deal.

*C gestures to the meatballs.*

C: *(To A)* Pass me that? I really shouldn't but they're just so delicious, aren't they?

A: Mm.

*A hands C the plate of meatballs. She spoons some onto her plate and passes it back to A, who puts it back in the middle of the table.*

B: Just be grateful you even got a raise. Not all of us got so lucky.

D: Grateful? I earned this and deserve it, thank you.

C: Of course you did!

D: It's like, do they even truly value me if they can't get this basic stuff right? If it were a one-off thing/

*B picks up his phone, waving it at D.*

B: *(to D)* Question: did they put that thing at the bottom of the email? "Sent from my iPhone, please excuse fat fingers." I love those. *(To A)* Give me a bit more of that would you?

*A spoons some meatballs onto B's plate gingerly.*

D: It's all so amusing to you. How do I explain this in terms you'll understand?

B: There's nothing to explain.

C: I wouldn't want to make a fuss. That's just me, though.

D: It's the principle.

B: You can't get fired for spelling someone's name wrong. Trust me, I've had the distinct privilege of being forced to read the employee handbook from back to front. Now if they'd/

C: Who's getting fired? You're not going to try and get them fired, are you?

D: Why not? That'd send a message. *(Beat)* Either I'm a dick or I suffer in silence. I can't win.

A: *(To D)* Can I just say that you are preaching to the choir. Well, at least a choir of one.

B: Here we go.

A: *(To D)* I wouldn't expect them to get it.

B: Get what?

A: You're just so white, that's all.

B: That's racist! You can't say that! Could you imagine if/

D  Is it 'preaching to the choir' or 'preaching to the congregation'? I never know which means what. *(To A)* You're saying you agree with me, right?

A: Yes, in the sense that/

C: *(Simultaneously)* It's choir.

B: *(Simultaneously)* It's congregation.

C: If you're preaching to the congregation, you're trying to convince them of something. If you're preaching to the choir, they're already in agreement with you. Thank you, Sunday school.

A: Come to think of it, it's a bit of a weird phrase, isn't it? I was in our school choir. But I definitely didn't always agree with the preaching.

B: <u>You</u> were in choir?

A: Yeah...

*A bursts into song to the tune of Guide Me, O Thou Great Redeemer (continues until his next line). "Guide me, O thou great redeemer, Pilgrim through this barren land; I am weak, but thou art mighty, Hold me with thy powerful hand; Bread of heaven, bread of heaven Feed me till I want no more; Feed me till I want no more."*

B: *(Overlapping)* Remember that guy in the year below who got out of going to church just because he was Jewish? So lucky.

A: You do know I'm not Jewish, right?

C: I think everyone can sort of decide for themselves, can't they?

D: That's a nice thought, but it doesn't really work like that in practice, because/

A: ...if everyone's doing things one way, and you're the odd one out/

D: It's hard enough without having to deal with all that.

C: I think schools these days cater for everyone. Or mine did at least.

A: Easy for you to say.

C: I love this place. The meatballs were <u>incredible</u>. *(To A)* Last one! It's all yours.

*C passes the serving spoon to A.*

*The scene freezes. A stands up, and walks slowly around the table. The others remain frozen. A regards the audience.*

A: I've spent the last three and a half years wondering about what happened that night. *(beat)* You recognise this situation, right? Maybe not. Well I'd been here many times before. This was familiar, almost verging on comfortable territory for me.

*A observes the situation around him.*

A: But this time around, things did not happen the way they usually did. How? That's what I'm still trying to figure out. Why? *(Pause.)* Here's the thing: I had so many ways I could have avoided it. Well-rehearsed white lies, oft-practiced stock responses, precision muscle memory. That night, it all seemed to go right out the window. *(Pause.)* When I try and make sense of it, I end up thinking about how else it might have gone, had I just...

*A takes his seat.*

A: You see, I had options. Option 1: "Just say no".

*Scene unfreezes.*

C: The meatballs were <u>incredible</u>. *(To A)* Last one! It's all yours.

*C passes the serving spoon to A.*

A: Oh, no thanks.

*A hands it back.*

C: You sure?

A: I'm so full.

*B reaches for the spoon.*

B: I'll have yours then.

*C bats his hand away. D looks up from her phone.*

D: This is impossible. I'm trying to find the sweet spot between 'don't fuck with me, I am a serious woman of business' and 'please understand that I very much want to keep my job.' *(Beat.)* Do people still say "To whom it may concern"?

B: Whom?

A: Yeah, I think that's right.

B: Who the fuck says whom?

C: Don't you mean "<u>whom</u> the fuck says whom?"

A: No, you certainly do not mean that.

B: I would never say whom. You'll sound like a wanker.

D: Well then, if you snobs wouldn't...

*D puts down her phone.*

D: Your school sounds like an interesting place. *(To A)* I hear you guys had quite the reputation.

A: Reputation?

B: Ah, the good old days.

A: *(To B)* Why do you sound like you're 75 years old? *(To D)* Truth be told, it's not something I look back on that fondly/

C: What do you mean? School was great!

A: I think that depends on how you look at it.

B: More wine? More wine, I think.

*B flings his arms around gesturing for a waiter.*

D: Listen: with all that education you've got, do you reckon you could at least <u>try</u> to pronounce Montepulciano correctly this time? What was it you said before? "Wont-ye-come-back-to-my-place-now?" Sounded like you were coming onto her.

B: Maybe I was.

D: There's not enough wine in the world to drown your lack of game.

C: *(To A)* Didn't I say she was great?

*(To D)* I've been telling him–

A: Yeah, it sort of seems like you replaced me.

C: Hey, you're the one who's been impossible to get a hold of.

A: We've all had stuff going on.

C: Well, yes of course, I'm not going to crucify you for that. And want to hear all about what you're up to, too. But first, you must try some of this, just a little bit. It's their signature.

*C picks up the meatball on the spoon, bringing it towards A's plate.*

A: I'm good, thanks.

C: *(To A)* To whom should your meatball go? To your mouth, methinks.

*C lifts the spoon towards A's mouth, meatball sauce dripping off it.*

A: ALRIGHT, PAUSE!

*Scene freezes. A gets up and addresses the audience.*

A: That's not how it went. But it could have. And what would I have done next? *(Beat.)* I guess I was resentful that they couldn't just… read my mind. Unfair and irrational of me, perhaps. Wasn't it obvious? And why was it that I always had to do the work of explaining myself? *(Beat.)* But, it's not like I hadn't done it before. *(Pause.)* Let's try this again.

*A snaps his fingers. B, C, and D all move in slow motion rewinding their actions to the point that it previously froze. A takes his seat.*

A: It didn't have to end the way it did. I still had options. Number two: "Be honest. They'll understand."

*Scene unfreezes.*

C: The meatballs were <u>incredible</u>. *(to A)* Last one! It's all yours.

A: Oh, I don't eat meatballs.

B: What?

A: You know that.

*A glares at B and C. D taps away at her phone.*

C: You don't? Of course you don't. To be honest, I shouldn't really either. I've been trying this new diet where I don't eat/

B: What do you mean you don't eat meatballs?

A: I don't eat pork, remember?

C: It's my mistake, I'm always getting these things mixed up... some of you it's no meat, some no pork/

A: Some of you?

C: Oh you know what I mean!

D: *(Without looking up from her phone)* My girlfriend doesn't eat pork. I've been dying to come here since it opened but haven't been able to.

C: *(To A.)* Remember the time your mum made us cottage pie?

A: Maybe... I'm not sure/

*C moves D's phone down from her face.*

C: *(To B and D.)* You'll love this. So, he was always banging on about how good of a cook his mum is. My mum's like, M&S, bish bash bosh, in the oven, done. So I'm always trying to get an invite round, and eventually, finally, I do! Only thing is, she's gone and made us COTTAGE PIE!

*Pause. B laughs hysterically, C joins in. D looks confused. A rolls his eyes.*

D: I don't get it. *(Picks up her phone again.)* Right guys, I'm doing this. If I copy in the managing partner, does that make me a grade A arsehole?

B: *(To C.)* Was it <u>so</u> disgusting?

C: No no no, it was… good! It's just, I was really looking forward to something authentic.

A: I didn't get why it was funny then and I'm still/

B: Because you're all excited and then it's like, "Where's the curry?"

C: Exactly!

B: At least you weren't on the shitter all night.

C: A blessing.

B: *(To A.)* So let me get this straight. Have you ever tried it?

A: Tried it?

B: Pork.

A: Have you ever seen me try it?

B: I think you should try it before saying you don't like it.

A: I didn't say I didn't like it. I said I don't eat it.

C: Why didn't you say something?

A: It's really not a big deal.

C: You know, they should have asked us about dietary requirements when they were taking our order.

A: It's not a problem, seriously.

*C looks around for a waiter.*

C: I should say something.

B: It's fine, you don't have to pay for them. But you should still try them. Don't worry about it.

A: I'm <u>not</u> worried about it.

*A takes a sip of wine.*

B: *(To D.)* He drinks, though.

> *D puts her phone down.*

D: Phew, there we go. I've sent it. Had to be done. *(Beat.)* What were you talking about?

> *B points at A.*

B: Says no to the meatballs but he won't say no to a glass of wine.

A: What's your point?

B: So you don't <u>really</u> care about this stuff then, do you?

> *B picks up the meatball on the spoon and stands up, gesturing towards A's face.*

Go on. I bet you'll love it.

> *A turns away.*

A: What are you playing at?

> *D laughs nervously. B walks around behind A and dangles the spoon in front of his mouth.*

B: Don't make a fuss.

D: *(To C.)* Is this some posh school thing I don't understand, like when they all jack off onto a biscuit?

A: Stop it.

> *B tries to open A's mouth with his hand.*

B: Now, now, don't get angry.

> *A tries to wriggle away.*

C: *(To D.)* It's just boys being boys.

*B has A in a choke-hold, his head arched backwards as if he's in a very aggressive dentist's chair.*

B: Come on.

A: I said stop.

*A bats B's hand away, knocking the meatball and sauce all over the table and C. C jumps. B backs up to his seat.*

B: Look what you've done. Spoilt a nice occasion.

*D's phone starts ringing. A jumps up and reaches towards C.*

A: *(To C)* I'm sorry, I – let me/

*C recoils. D's phone continues to ring.*

C: Just leave it.

D: Shit, it's the office. I'd better take this.

*D stands and starts to leave the table. Scene freezes. A stands up and cleans himself off. He regards the audience.*

A: Not great, right? Looking back, I suppose I had decided that it just wasn't the night to risk this particular disaster.

*A climbs onto his chair.*

A: It was tiring always being the odd one out. Tiring, having to repeat myself, time after time after… hadn't I told them this before? *(Beat)* Maybe I was more tired than usual.

*A snaps his fingers and jumps down from his chair. B, C, and D rewind their positions back to the start of the play.*

Maybe I couldn't face being told I was a hypocrite, or not that night at least. Trust me, I was self-conscious enough trying to figure this whole thing out, explaining things to myself, to…

*A takes his seat. The scene unfreezes. B, C, and D resume eating and drinking. This time, the action at the table takes place as if A was watching a silent movie around him. He's at the same meal, but the others don't see or acknowledge his presence.*

A: The truth is, I still don't know how, or why, or… whether it was one thing, or anything. It just happened.

*A looks at each person around the table in turn, then back to the plate of meatballs.*

A: It was so out of character. Something that had never happened before, never since, maybe never again.

*A slowly spoons one large meatball onto his plate, tucks his napkin back in. He cuts the meatball.*

A: If nobody noticed, did it even happen? I'm not sure if there's such a thing as 'Schrodinger's meatball'.

*A lifts his fork towards his mouth, staring at it.*

A: It's hard to explain, really.

*A slowly puts the meatball into his mouth. Lights down as he closes his mouth around his fork.*

## END

WHEN THE LEAVES FALL
BY GRACE TARR

# Character List

SHAY. (FEMALE, 23-25) *Mixed-race*
Very chatty, would rather talk than have silence.
Nervous. Shay hates letting people down and
cares a lot about what others think. Only child
and looks after her mother. Politically and
environmentally conscious. New environmental
activist.

BILLIE. (FEMALE, 23-25) *No specific ethnicity*
Quiet, thoughtful and compassionate. Picks
words carefully and is aware of how her actions
affect others. Environmental activist.

MAX. (MALE, 27-29) *No specific ethnicity*
Billie's elder sibling. Sharp, task focused and
doesn't react well to situations he is not in
control of. Strong political and environmental
beliefs.

*Note on Text*
… indicates a slight break in the dialogue.

/ indicates when one person interrupts another.

There are times when both characters will be
speaking at the same time, this is indicated.

*Setting*
A forest. Near a large city.

*Night.*

*A clearing in a forest. It's autumn. There are leaves on the floor. There are two bikes, a large duffle bag and two smaller backpacks.*

*Two people are sat on the floor of the forest, they're young. 20's. BILLIE, is on her back reading from a note book with a pen in her mouth and staring at the sky. SHAY, is smoking and holding her phone. It's quiet.*

SHAY: What can you see?

BILLIE: Orion's belt, I think.

SHAY: Where?

BILLIE: There.

SHAY: I can't. Oh, yeah… It's bigger than I thought. Didn't think I'd see this many stars so close to home.

BILLIE: They're there, you just gotta be in the right place.

*Pause.*

SHAY: My Mum… she loves the cranes at night. From our old flat you could see all the red dots that mark the top of them and, and she'd say they were her stars.

*SHAY puts out the cigarette and lies down next to BILLIE.*

BILLIE: You cold?

SHAY: Yeaaah. *(Pause.)* When, when's your brother getting here?

BILLIE: Max'll be here at 11, maybe later.

SHAY: Okay.

BILLIE: Do you have another coat or something?

SHAY: No. I'll be alright.

BILLIE: You didn't bring a lot with you. I can get him to bring you another coat, or a scarf, just something else to keep you warm?

SHAY: I'll be alright.

BILLIE: You can always use my sleeping bag as a blanket/

SHAY: I'm fine… Thanks.

*Pause.*

Ah, ah. A shooting star?

BILLIE: Where?

SHAY: There, there. Look.

BILLIE: Where?

SHAY: There.

BILLIE: No. It can't be.

SHAY: What is it?

BILLIE: It's a plane.

*SHAY laughs.*

SHAY: Oh, I was gonna make a wish.

*SHAY's stomach rumbles. She laughs.*

SHAY: Sorry. I did eat.

BILLIE: Stomach sounds hungry.

*SHAY laughs.*

Oh, and I think I have Oreos, if you want some?

SHAY: Uh, yeah. Please.

*BILLIE gets an Oreo packet out. SHAY eats quickly.*

SHAY: Do you eat the cream or the biscuit first?

BILLIE: Biscuit.

SHAY: I'm cream.

BILLIE: Otherwise it's too dry… I'm writing, have written something. Something new. *(Pause.)* It's short. But it's called 'Flying her home' I think.

SHAY: You want me to read it?

BILLIE: Yeah. I might change the title.

*BILLIE gives SHAY her note book.*

BILLIE: Yeah. Here. It's not finished.

SHAY: You gonna perform it tomorrow?

BILLIE: Haven't decided yet.

SHAY: *(Reading.)* 'I saw through'

BILLIE: No! Don't. Read it in your head.

SHAY: Right.

*Shay reads as BILLIE watches intently.*

SHAY: It's good. I get what you mean about the title… but I like it.

BILLIE: Thanks.

SHAY: It's really, really good. They all are. *(Starts flicking though BILLIE's note book.)* You know we should really start filming these. When you perform them. Put them up. They'd get loads of views.

BILLIE: I like that they're one-offs. You know, only the people who are there really get it.

43

SHAY: I know. I just think you could do more with them, reach more people. Like the people who don't come to protests. You know?

*BILLIE lies back watching the stars again. SHAY watches her. Silence.*

SHAY: Billie.

BILLIE: Hm.

SHAY: How d'you get people to listen… to you?

BILLIE: What?

SHAY: People talk over me a lot… *(Pause.)* Maybe it's because of my voice or that I'm female, or maybe it's just that they don't like what I'm saying.

*Pause.*

But it's different when you're performing, people listen to you.

BILLIE: Who's not listening to you?

SHAY: No one. That wasn't what I…

*Pause.*

SHAY: It's so quiet.

BILLIE: Hm.

*Pause.*

SHAY: Billie.

BILLIE: Hm.

SHAY: You're not going to sleep?

BILLIE: No.

*Silence.*

SHAY: *(Sighs.)* There's so much air. *(Takes a deep breath in.)*

BILLIE: *(Laughs.)*

SHAY: It's different right?

BILLIE: *(Laughs.)*

SHAY: It is... Go on. Take a deep breath with me. Pretend you're in a yoga class.

*They breath in.*

SHAY: You have to say it's different. It's like the air I normally breath isn't air. Like I was breathing, dirt. Now I'm taking my first breaths and I just want to... Ugh. Do you ever feel like that? So... you, you just want to...

*SHAY stands and lets out an almighty howl. It's almost a cry.*

*BILLIE looks at her, laughs and joins in.*

SHAY: I'm a wolf.

*Pause. Breathing. Howls again.*

SHAY: A werewolf. Awoooooooooooooooooooooo.

BILLIE: You're more of a puppy.

*SHAY grabs and licks BILLIE's face.*

BILLIE: You're disgusting.

*Pause.*

SHAY: Time?

BILLIE: It's five to eleven.

SHAY: *(Pause.)* You're not talking today. *(Pause.)* That's not a bad thing, just like an observation. I, I'm finding myself filling the silences/

BILLIE: You don't have to.

SHAY: I know. Words just keep coming out my mouth.

*SHAY lights another cigarette. Offers BILLIE it.*

BILLIE: Quitting.

SHAY: Right, sorry. Forgot….

BILLIE: You should really quit, smoking is bad on so may levels/not only what it does to you but the…

SHAY: I know. Yes. Bad person right here!

BILLIE: That's not what I meant.

SHAY: It is what you said though.

BILLIE: Right.

SHAY: Tomorrow… You should let me film you.

BILLIE: I'll think about it.

SHAY: I'll only put it up if you say it's okay.

*SHAY's phone beeps.*

BILLIE: Okay?

SHAY: Yeah! Sorry, it's Mum.

*SHAY texts. Silence.*

BILLIE: She okay?

SHAY: Hm, yeah. Sorry, it's away.

BILLIE: It's good.

*SHAY puts her phone away. Silence.*

SHAY: What if it doesn't do anything?

BILLIE: What?

SHAY: Tomorrow.

*Pause.*

BILLIE: What's going on? *(Pause.)* Shay.

SHAY: Nothing.

BILLIE: If it mobilises one more person then it's done something.

SHAY: Yeah… yeah. There is just this… this feeling. It's kinda over, UH overwhel… I feel like it's not enough.

BILLIE: I don't think there is such a thing as enough. It's about doing what you can.

SHAY: I know, I know. I feel, like I, I've not done anything and, I mean I know I've done things. It it, just feels like no matter how much I try to do or want to do it's, ah. Oh. It's, it's never enough. And I know you can't quantify what enough really is. But… Do you get what I'm trying to say? It's like every step I take someone else is taking 10 in the wrong direction. My actions will never, never ever be enough and, and there are only 100 companies that make up the 70% of the worlds $CO_2$ emissions. There are over 7 billion people in the world and only 100 companies that, that have fucked us. And continue to fuck us on a daily basis and, and I. All, all the information, it, it feels paralysing. What is me/

BILLIE: Wait, stop. Shay. Is this/

SHAY: No matter what I do it effects someone else's life negatively, if I buy an avocado, or quinoa, or use gas to cook in my house, or brush my teeth with the tap running. I have… there are issues… if I am ….

BILLIE: It's not about one person's actions, it's about the companies responsible taking/

SHAY: And I keep thinking... I, I can't be the only one/

BILLIE: I don't think you are/

SHAY: But I feel like I... It's all... it all just feels never enough, never ever enough. It will never be enough and, and that, that is pushing me towards doing things I... I shouldn't, no, things I wouldn't normally do. I know this isn't a normal thing. I just, I, I'm terrified to go tomorrow.

*Silence.*

SHAY: I'm fucking scared... and my Mum keeps saying I'm gonna get arrested and that's permanent. That could permanently affect my life.

*Silence.*

BILLIE: Right. Your Mum, she/

SHAY: She was reading an article, the people who were in the climate protest in Paris, the police covered them in tear gas and used batons. It was a peaceful protest and.... On that day over 150 people were arrested.

BILLIE: Good... Well not good that the police used excessive force on non-violent civil disobedience which is reprehensible and immoral... But, people need to be arrested.

SHAY: She started crying and begging me not to come tonight.

BILLIE: I'm sorry...

*Pause.*

BILLIE: People do need to take this seriously... I think being arrested is important.

SHAY: Billie.

BILLIE: It makes an actual point. I want to be arrested. I want to go to court and stand in-front of the judge and I want to ask them, I mean why else do you become a judge if you don't want to serve justice and what is going on isn't just, it's ecocide. I want to tell them/

SHAY: You can't just tell a judge/

BILLIE: Yes I can/. I'm gonna tell the judge

SHAY: That's not how it works/

BILLIE: I'm gonna tell the judge what's going on and/

SHAY: You can't do that.

BILLIE: Yes I can. I've pre-written it./

SHAY: No you can't.

BILLIE: I know exactly what I am going to say.

SHAY: What if you make the judge angry? What if they don't like being challenged?

BILLIE: Then they are the people who need challenging.

SHAY: We can't force change.

BILLIE: No that's exactly what we can do. That's what we have to do. We have to get up off our arses and force change.

*Silence.*

BILLIE: Paris was different. That's not gonna happen tomorrow, the police here/

SHAY: Billie, listen to yourself…. The way we are going. It feels like people are going to get hurt.

BILLIE: Shay/

SHAY: Don't… that's what happens.

BILLIE: What's what happens?

SHAY: People, people. The suffragettes, they got the 3.5% but in the process, the woman at the races. Fine it started with arrests and then prison sentencing but then people died.

BILLIE: You're overthinking this.

SHAY: Yes I am. But what am I supposed to do? I have all this information spinning around in my head and I'm seeing it all and, and… that's the way it's going.

BILLIE: That won't happen tomorrow.

SHAY: I'm not saying it will. But if we keep accelerating at this pace in six months, a year maybe… It's already happened, when David Buckel set himself on fire. He burnt himself alive because he genuinely believed that was the only way to create real change.

BILLIE: He was an ill/

SHAY: And this, the sacrifices people are making may not even make a difference.

BILLIE: You can't think like that… We can't think like that. Look this is not the point. Tomorrow's action… It is our democratic right to protest.

SHAY: They won't see this as a protest.

BILLIE: It's non-violent Shay.

SHAY: They'll see it as an attack.

BILLIE: It's not an attack… But if it wakes 'them' up, then good.

SHAY: No, no. Not good, waking 'them' leads/ to

BILLIE: Yes, good, we need the pigs who sit in our government to look up from their little bubbles, to stop dragging their feet and to stop putting their wallets first. Action needs to be taken to make that happen.

SHAY: And you're willing to do it?

MAX: *(Off.)* Billie. BILLIE.

BILLIE: Shay.

SHAY: I can't do it.

*A torch light swings across the stage.*

BILLIE: HERE. We're here.

*MAX enters. Runs and spins BILLIE around.*

MAX: Ready?

BILLIE: Yeaaah.

MAX: Hey Shay.

MAX hugs her.

MAX: You good?

SHAY: Yeah.

MAX: Do you want a hand with your bag?

SHAY: No.

MAX: Oh, how much do I owe you for the shop?

SHAY: It was £20/

MAX: Right, can I/

SHAY: But it's fine, Billie paid for it.

MAX: Great. And it's in here?

BILLIE: Yeah.

*MAX goes over to the duffel bag and looks inside. SHAY goes to get her bike.*

BILLIE: Are you gonna come?

SHAY: No.

BILLIE: What's going on?

SHAY: Nothing. I'm just not okay with this anymore/

BILLIE: Why?

*MAX is watching them.*

MAX: What's going on?/ *(Pause.)* Are you leaving?

SHAY: Nothing.

BILLIE: We haven't finished talking Shay. What's happen/

SHAY: NOTHING.

MAX: Is she not coming?

BILLIE: Shay. Look at me.

MAX: What about tomorrow?

*Silence.*

BILLIE: Shay/

SHAY: I can't.

MAX: Okay…

BILLIE: Okay.

SHAY: I'm sorry.

BILLIE: It's fine.

MAX: I'm confused.

*Pause.*

SHAY: I don't, I'm not comfortable.

MAX: Why?

*Pause.*

SHAY: I'm worried about/

MAX: There's nothing to worry about.

SHAY: I want to go home Max.

MAX: Why?

SHAY: I don't. I need to go home. I'm... I...

BILLIE: It's okay.

MAX: No, it's not okay. Shay, what's going on?

SHAY: I can't afford to get/

MAX: Can't afford what?

SHAY: Isn't there a halfway? *(Pause.)* Surely there is something/

MAX: What?

SHAY: Something other than stopping a/

MAX: We are collapsing. People have known about the greenhouse effect since 1824. They've done nothing. It's not about mitigation. The governments and fossil fuel industry leaders have/

BILLIE: Max please don't start/

MAX: Since 1990 CO2 emissions have gone up 60%. And they're still rising. This is the 6th mass extinction. 1 million species are currently threatened with extinction. Sea levels are rising.

SHAY: Why are you talking like this?/

BILLIE: You sound like Dad.

MAX: If we have a two metre sea level rise it could displace 180 million people. 180 million. Where are these people going to go? That is what your 'halfway' gets; social collapse, climate breakdown and all in our brainwashed need to value convenience, consumption and exploitation/ over, over life.

SHAY: I know all this. I know these facts. I know this. And it gnaws at me everyday. It/

MAX: It's not enough for you to be sad about it.

BILLIE: Can you not Ma/

MAX: We are facing mass starvation in the next 10 years because of the collapse in the weather systems around the world. It's not enough for her to just feel it, it's not enough to say that she is sad about it. The science is real. We have to make people tell the truth.

SHAY: I know the truth. I'm just/

BILLIE: It's okay/

SHAY: I just need to know that tomorrow is gonna make an actual difference. What we are doing isn't just gonna disrupt people's holidays. That it's gonna/

BILLIE: You don't have to come with us.

SHAY: Thank/

MAX: Yes she does. Billie, you can't commit to bringing people along if they are gonna back out hours before. Do you understand what position that puts me in? Do you get that that's not okay?

SHAY: She is not bringing me along. I made the decision to come, things have changed and now I can't.

MAX: What's changed?

BILLIE: Shay?

*Pause.*

SHAY: I don't need to explain myself.

MAX: Will you still come if I can guarantee you won't be arrested?

BILLIE: You can't guarantee that.

MAX: Let her answer. Will you?

*Silence.*

MAX: Shay, I can/

SHAY: You can't guarantee that.

MAX: No, I can. Our relationship with the police/

SHAY: Relationship? Max, you cannot guarantee anything. It is naive to think you have any relationship with the/

MAX: Naive. Doing nothing is naive.

SHAY: I'm not doing nothing/

MAX: We have to get to Net Zero in the next 6 years to prevent more that two degree warming. This has to happen or we will hit a tipping point and there will be no going back. Right now 200 species are going extinct everyday/

BILLIE: Talk to her like a person Max not like you're giving a ted talk/

MAX: Everyday.... I don't want to upset you. Relationship was the wrong word to use. I, just.... Look. You have the choice right here, you have a choice to be overwhelmed and to freak out and worry or you can act and through that action, through acting and creating change the fear it, it dissipates. Please.... Shay.... Stop fucking looking at me and say something.

BILLIE: Max!

MAX: Sorry... I, we need you tomorrow. We need everyone. It has to be every type... Everyone. I, we need it to be everyone. To make change. This is...This is everything. I, this is. I, we need this to be successful.

*MAX takes hold of SHAY.*

SHAY: Don't touch me.

MAX: It can't business as usual anymore. The elites are taking us to our death. To our death.

BILLIE: Stop it.

MAX: We are going to die if we don't/

SHAY: Shut up!

BILLIE: Max!

MAX: It's the truth.

SHAY: Doing this is too much for me/I didn't grow up like you did.

MAX: The truth is too much?

SHAY: I am happy to protest, I will be at every People's Assembly possible. I'm not comfortable putting my safety at stake and yours, Billie, this is dangerous/

MAX: This is no more dangerous than blocking a road.

SHAY: Noo. It is. Then, I can get up and move if asked. In the middle of a road I have tonnes of ways to evade contact with the police. Here, you haven't given me a choice.

MAX: You agreed to this. This is not something new that's just been thrust upon you, Shay.

SHAY: You're not listening to me.

MAX: Because you're not making sense. You keep saying you can't but you're not explaining yourself.

SHAY: I don't have to Max.

MAX: Whatever I say you're gonna disagree with me. You're acting like a child/

BILLIE: I think that's enough Max.

MAX: She needs to understand she can't change her mind/

SHAY: Will you stop talking about me as though I'm not here.

MAX: You're a fucking coward/ you

SHAY: What will be enough for you Max? Huh? What do I have to do that will be enough for you? Tell me. Do you want me to b/

MAX: It's bullsh/

SHAY: I can't make anymore sacrifices.

*Pause.*

MAX: We have to leave.

*MAX gathers his bags.*

BILLIE: Go, I'll catch you up.

*MAX exits.*

BILLIE: Once… once we start acting hope will come.

*Silence.*

BILLIE: Tomorrow will go as planned. I thought you were happy… you know what we said we'd do. I'm not asking anything more of you than you already agreed.

SHAY: I'm not allowed to change my mind?

BILLIE: You are…

*Pause.*

BILLIE: Are you okay?

*Pause..*

BILLIE: I'm, I'm scared too. I'm scared this won't be enough. But I have to do something. I have to do everything I can. I have to do everything I can.

SHAY: I can't do this… My Mum… she. If I got arrested…

BILLIE: Shay, is your Mum doing okay?

SHAY: Yeah. She's fine.

*Pause. BILLIE embraces SHAY. Knowing that she is lying.*

SHAY: Please be careful.

BILLIE: I will.

SHAY: The pol/

BILLIE: I know… I'm sorry Max.. he…. I'll come find you when I get back. Okay?

SHAY: Yeah.

*BILLIE kisses SHAY goodbye. It's not romantic, it's kindness. SHAY watches BILLIE exit.*

*Lights down.*

ONE OF THE GOOD ONES
BY VIVIAN XIE

# Character List

ELAINE CHAO
United States Secretary of Transportation.
Republican. 40+, Taiwanese.

MITCH MCCONNELL
United States Senate Majority Leader.
Republican. 40+, Caucasian.

*Late night, Washington D.C. McConnell family home.*

*ELAINE CHAO, United States Secretary of Transportation, scrolls through Tweets and sips on tea. She taps on a video.*

PROTESTOR: *(Video.)* Why are you separating families at the border? Why are you separating families?

ELAINE: *(Video.)* Why don't you leave my husband alone? Leave my husband alone! He's not!

PROTESTOR: *(Video.)* How does he sleep at night?! How does he sleep at night?!

*Her husband Senate Majority Leader MITCH MCCONNELL enters.*

MITCH: Not watching that again, are you?

ELAINE: I thought you went to bed.

MITCH: Can't sleep.

This damn news cycle…

*He looks outside the window.*

MITCH: There's that damn guy from The Post again.

How am I supposed to lead tomorrow's debate with him taking photos every time I change sleeping positions?

And who the hell schedules Senate meetings at 6 in the morning?

ELAINE: Calm down. Tea?

MITCH: Sure.

ELAINE: Gerard's gone home for the weekend. Kettle's downstairs.

MITCH: Don't know why we have a butler if he isn't around to butler.

ELAINE: We're out of decaf Earl Grey.

MITCH: Is that all we have?

ELAINE: There's a box of breakfast tea.

MITCH: …forget it. I don't want any tea anymore.

ELAINE: Okay.

MITCH: Turn that off.

ELAINE: It's just a video.

MITCH: I look like an idiot.

ELAINE: No you don't.

MITCH: I don't like it.

ELAINE: You're being paranoid.

MITCH: Whoever filmed it, they make me look like a…a…

ELAINE: What?

*He whips out his own phone and scrolls through tweets.*

ELAINE: No wonder you can't sleep if you're scrolling through tweets in bed.

MITCH: Look, listen to this one: "Two thoughts: 1. Elaine Chao is a bad ass. 2. A bunch of white guys harassing an Asian woman is not a good look." A bunch of white guys. I mean, what does that make me?

ELAINE: They don't mean you. Get off, Twitter isn't good for you.

MITCH: I don't harass you.

ELAINE: You don't.

MITCH: You paused.

ELAINE: I did not.

MITCH: Do I harass you?

ELAINE: Not usually.

MITCH: Usually?

ELAINE: Well right now, you're being a little-/

MITCH: Oh sorry. Didn't know talking to my wife constituted harassment. Like normal couples do.

ELAINE: For God's sake, Mitch. Just ignore them.

MITCH: How am I supposed to ignore them? Look, this one's from the NRA: "This is how the violent left treats Secretary Elaine Chao. An immigrant. The first Asian America woman and the first Chinese America to serve as a Cabinet member in American history. Don't be fooled." The NRA! They're our biggest lobbyists!

The press will have a field day with that one...

ELAINE: "Chinese America"? You mean Chinese American?

MITCH: No. They wrote "Chinese America". "The first Asian America woman and the first Chinese America".

ELAINE: Huh.

MITCH: These people are so hung up about where everyone's from. Immigrant this and immigrant that.

Do they have to mention it every time? Sure your parents are Chinese but-/

ELAINE: They're Taiwanese.

MITCH: And you're American. The papers keep making you look like an immigrant.

ELAINE: But I am an immigrant. I was born in Taiwan.

MITCH: You know what I mean.

ELAINE: No.

MITCH: You know…

ELAINE: I was born in Taiwan.

MITCH: But you're not like an immigrant-immigrant.

ELAINE: Immigrant-immigrant.

MITCH: Yeah.

ELAINE: You mean I'm a good immigrant?

MITCH: Exactly.

ELAINE: Not an illegal immigrant?

MITCH: Sure. Whatever.

ELAINE: Good to know.

MITCH: Nothing about me, nothing about how I was literally attacked by a bunch of thugs.

ELAINE: We weren't attacked.

MITCH: Sure I was.

ELAINE: Nobody laid a hand on us.

MITCH: Well I felt attacked.

ELAINE: They weren't that bad.

MITCH: Easy for you to say. Everyone thinks you're a hero now.

ELAINE: Hm.

MITCH: What does that mean?

ELAINE: What?

MITCH: What does that mean?

ELAINE: What does what mean?

MITCH: You know…

ELAINE: Mitch, it is too late at night to play this game. I'm going to bed.

MITCH: What does "hm" mean?

ELAINE: It just means…hm. Like…okay. Interesting idea. That's all.

*Pause.*

MITCH: You're enjoying this.

ELAINE: Enjoying what?

MITCH: This. The video. The tweets. All of it.

ELAINE: I'm not enjoying anything.

MITCH: You like looking like a hero. The quiet, Asian woman defending her man. It's just your type of feminism.

ELAINE: Nobody said that.

MITCH: Nobody has to.

ELAINE: Well, you're free to think whatever you want.

*MITCH scrolls through more tweets as he brings the kettle to the table.*

MITCH: "Get you someone like that turtle-lipped bitch somehow has Elaine Chao."

I swear to high heaven, if I ever meet Jon Stewart I will kill him.

*MITCH begins typing.*

ELAINE: Christ, don't tweet back.

MITCH: I don't like it.

ELAINE: You don't like a lot of things. Doesn't mean you need to respond.

And you won't be able to hold the Senate floor tomorrow if the press is breathing down your neck about some stupid tweet.

Be better than them.

MITCH: They're saying you faked the video.

ELAINE: What?

MITCH: "Wife of Senator Mitch McConnell, Elaine Chao, Secretary of Transportation, accused of faking confrontational video".

ELAINE: Who's saying that?

MITCH: CNN.

ELAINE: Hm.

MITCH: There it is again! What does that mean?

ELAINE: It doesn't mean anything!

MITCH: It sounds like you mean "I'm not listening, Mitch. I don't really care, Mitch. Shut up, Mitch!"

ELAINE: It means "I don't like what that tweet is saying, Mitch. Let me think for a second, Mitch. Stop being so sensitive, Mitch!"

*Pause.*

ELAINE: People will tweet what they want. Our job is to ignore them. We don't need to engage.

MITCH: What happened to "leave my husband alone" Elaine?

The one so keen to defend her poor, helpless husband?

ELAINE: Twitter fights are for the foolish who enjoy the performance of their own politics.

MITCH: Very poetic. Almost like you rehearsed it.

ELAINE: Oh for God's sake. If you're not going to sleep, then I am.

MITCH: God, it'd be a hundred times worse if it were staged.

ELAINE: Well it wasn't staged. Good night.

MITCH: Of course it wasn't.

*Silence.*

MITCH: Can't have been.

*Silence.*

MITCH: Was it?

ELAINE: No.

MITCH: Elaine!

ELAINE: It wasn't!

MITCH: Did you fake that video?

ELAINE: No!

MITCH: It all makes sense now. Those men knew exactly which exit we were going to take.

ELAINE: Mitch-

MITCH: All the facts line up and point at you. What those men said, how they knew where we were going to be, and at what time too!

ELAINE: Well, you're free to think whatever you want.

MITCH: I'm thinking I know the truth about my wife now.

ELAINE: What you think and what the truth is are two wildly different things, Mitch.

MITCH: I know you think I'm an idiot, but I know some things.

ELAINE: I've never said you're an idiot.

You were there. You have the video. Does it look like it's being faked?

MITCH: I don't know. Is it fake? You sure look like you knew what you were doing, charging in on them like that. How much did you pay those guys, huh? Did you tell them to chant? Or would that have been extra? Where do you even hire actors like that? Don't tell me, you had some people over at Wells Fargo pull some wages for you to pay them off. Or let me guess, you-/

ELAINE: Fine! I paid them. You caught me. Happy?

*Silence.*

MITCH: Stop joking, Elaine. This is serious.

ELAINE: I'm not joking.

MITCH: You paid them.

ELAINE: Yes.

MITCH: Is that really what you think of me?

ELAINE: Apparently you know exactly what I think now.

MITCH: Why would you do it, Elaine? Do you have any idea what this is going to do to me? To us?

ELAINE: Why do we do anything? Why does anybody in D.C. do anything?

MITCH: How am I supposed to explain this to people at work tomorrow?

ELAINE: Not my problem, is it...

MITCH: And to think, you used the immigration issue against me.

ELAINE: Don't be dramatic.

MITCH: You know I don't want to separate families? If they'd just come through properly-

ELAINE: I didn't tell them what to say, Mitch. Next week it'll be about the gays.

MITCH: Oh so you're already planning one for next week-/

ELAINE: No, I'm just saying you can't believe-/

MITCH: Oh yes, tell me more about what you think-/

ELAINE: I was just getting things done-/

MITCH: You made me look like an absolute fool-/

ELAINE: Grow up-/

MITCH: Grow up? You, the one who faked a viral video, are telling me to grow up?

I have to get on the Senate floor tomorrow and get everyone to agree to another immigration ban while you're sucking off frat boys.

ELAINE: I gave you an opportunity to be a man and confront those boys and you ran straight for the car. What was I supposed to do? I made you look a fool? I can't make you something you already are!

*Beat.*

MITCH: Well. Glad to know you think I'm a coward.

ELAINE: Glad to let you know.

MITCH: My god, Elaine. What are we doing?

If you really think of me like this then why don't we just-

*MITCH stops himself.*

ELAINE: Don't even say it.

MITCH: I didn't.

ELAINE: You're not divorcing me.

MITCH: Maybe…we should.

ELAINE: If anybody is divorcing, I'd divorce you.

MITCH: This isn't about semantics, goddammit. This is our marriage!

ELAINE: Marriage is semantics! You really believe getting married is about love? Everything about it lies in what we say!

In the words we vowed to one another! In every single detail, everything about this relationship, about our jobs, about us, is semantics!

The power of everything we do lies in the details. You should know, you run the damn Senate!

MITCH: So…that's what this is all about.

ELAINE: What?

MITCH: Its power lies in the details…

ELAINE: What are you on about?

MITCH: Those men weren't there for me. They were there for you.

*Silence.*

MITCH: Why did you marry me?

*Silence.*

MITCH: Do I make you look powerful?

*ELAINE sips her tea.*

MITCH: Do I make you feel powerful?

ELAINE: I'm going to bed.

MITCH: I'm just asking my wife a very simple question.

ELAINE: Nothing is simple, Mitch.

MITCH: After what you did to us, this should be.

*Silence.*

ELAINE: I took the last Earl Grey.

You can have some of mine if you want.

MITCH: You're not going to deny anything?

ELAINE: Will it change anything?

MITCH: It might. If it were for the right reasons.

ELAINE: …do you want me to apologize?

MITCH: Will it change anything?

ELAINE: I don't know. I just…

MITCH: What?

ELAINE: I feel-/

MITCH: Guilty?

ELAINE: Not exactly.

MITCH: What then?

ELAINE: Like I should apologize. If that's what normal couples do.

If that's what you want me to do.

I'm going to have to anyway.

*Pause.*

*MITCH exits.*

*He returns with a mug of tea, the box of Earl Grey. The Earl Grey is empty. He tosses it in the rubbish.*

MITCH: Weren't lying about that one.

ELAINE: Mitch. Please.

MITCH: Why'd you leave the box in the cupboard?

*MITCH begins drinking his own mug of tea.*

ELAINE: It's late. You have to get up early and I now have to draft an apology. We should get some sleep.

…I won't say what you want me to say.

MITCH: …I know.

ELAINE: Yes.

MITCH: …yes.

ELAINE: We shouldn't act now.

MITCH: Yes.

ELAINE: In two years, perhaps.

MITCH: Very analytical.

ELAINE: Unfortunately, yes.

MITCH: And tomorrow's news cycle?

ELAINE: …that's tomorrow's problem.

*Pause.*

*They drink their tea. Mitch cringes at his.*

ELAINE: Did you make yours too strong?

Here.

*ELAINE and MITCH share her tea, scrolling through their phones.*

MITCH: Looks like our man wants another Muslim ban.

ELAINE: Good.

That's good.

Printed in the USA
CPSIA information can be obtained
at www.ICGtesting.com
LVHW020859171024
794056LV00002B/629

9 781786 829207